D1384993

The Inside Story
Skyscraper

Dana Meachen Rau

Marshall Cavendish
Benchmark
New York

Inside a Skyscraper

1 core

2 piles

3 rock

4 steel beams

5 windows

5

1

4

Marion Public Library
1095 6th Avenue
Marion, Iowa 52302-3428
(319) 377-3412

2

3

You see a lot of tall buildings in a city.

Skyscrapers seem to touch the sky.

Many people live and work in skyscrapers.

Some skyscrapers have more than 100 floors.

To build a skyscraper, workers clear a big space.

They dig in the ground until they find rock.

Rock is strong.

It will hold up the skyscraper.

Workers put *piles* into the ground.

Piles are legs that the skyscraper stands on.

Above the ground, workers build with *steel beams*.

Tall cranes lift the beams.

Steel beams go side to side.

Steel posts hold up the beams.

Workers build a hard *core*.

The core keeps the skyscraper steady.

On the outside, workers put on stone or metal.

They put in many windows.

On the inside, workers build floors and walls.

They paint and put in lights.

How can you get from the bottom to the top?

Elevators bring you from floor to floor.

All skyscrapers are tall.

Skyscrapers can be higher than the clouds.

Inside a Skyscraper

core

elevator

piles

steel beams

walls

windows

Challenge Words

core (KOR) The middle.

elevators (EL-uh-vayt-uhrs) Machines that carry people up and down.

piles Strong posts in the ground that hold up a skyscraper.

steel beams (BEEMS) Heavy, long pieces of strong metal.

29

Index

Page numbers in **boldface** are illustrations.

About the Author

Dana Meachen Rau is an author, editor, and illustrator. A graduate of Trinity College in Hartford, Connecticut, she has written more than one hundred fifty books for children, including nonfiction, biographies, early readers, and historical fiction. She lives with her family in Burlington, Connecticut.

Reading Consultants

Nanci Vargus, Ed.D. is an Assistant Professor of Elementary Education at the University of Indianapolis.

Beth Walker Gambro received her M.S. Ed. Reading from the University of St. Francis, Joliet, Illinois.

With thanks to Nanci Vargus, Ed.D. and Beth Walker Gambro, reading consultants

Marshall Cavendish Benchmark
Marshall Cavendish
99 White Plains Road
Tarrytown, New York 10591-9001
www.marshallcavendish.us

Library of Congress Cataloging-in-Publication Data

Rau, Dana Meachen, 1971–
Skyscraper / by Dana Meachen Rau.
p. cm. — (Bookworms: the inside story)
Summary: "Describes the architecture, construction, and interior
of a skyscraper"—Provided by publisher.
Includes index.
ISBN-13: 978-0-7614-2276-1
ISBN-10: 0-7614-2276-5
1. Skyscrapers—Juvenile literature. I. Title. II. Series.
NA6230.R38 2006
720'.483—dc22
2005029850

Photo Research by Anne Burns Images

Cover Photo by Corbis/Alan Schein Photography

The photographs in this book are used with permission and through the courtesy of:
Corbis: pp. 1, 5, 13, 25, 28br Alan Schein Photography; pp. 21, 29tl Bill Varle;
pp. 23, 28tr Caroline/zefa; p. 27 Lester Lefkowitz. *The Image Works*: pp. 7, 9, 15, 17, 19, 28tl, 29tr
Michael J. Doolittle. *Photri-Microstock*: pp. 11, 28bl.

Printed in Malaysia
1   3   5   6   4   2

0000211320480